INSTRUMENTS in MUSIC

RELIGIOUS MUSIC

Roger Thomas

First published in Great Britain by Heinemann Library
Halley Court, Jordan Hill, Oxford OX2 8EJ
a division of Reed Educational and Professional Publishing Ltd.
Heinemann is a registered trademark of Reed Educational and Professional Publishing Ltd.

OXFORD FLORENCE PRAGUE MADRID ATHENS
MELBOURNE AUCKLAND KUALA LUMPUR SINGAPORE TOKYO
IBADAN NAIROBI KAMPALA JOHANNESBURG GABORONE
PORTSMOUTH NH (USA) CHICAGO MEXICO CITY SAO PAULO

Designed by Susan Clarke
Printed in Hong Kong

02 01 00 99 98
10 9 8 7 6 5 4 3 2 1

ISBN 0 431 08809 8

British Library Cataloguing in Publication Data

Thomas, Roger
  Religious music. – (Instruments in music)
  1.Church music – Juvenile literature 2.Music – Religious aspects –
  Juvenile literature 3.Musical instruments – Juvenile literature
  I.Title
  781.4'17

Acknowledgements
The Publishers would like to thank the following for permission to reproduce photographs:
Andes Press Agency, pp.4, 6, 8, 9, 19 (Carlos Reyes-Manzo); Circa Photo Library, p.13; Trevor
Clifford, p.17 top left, top centre, bottom left, p.27 left, top left, top right, right (John Myatt
Brass and Woodwind), p.17 top right and bottom right, p.27 centre bottom (Parker Brass);
Corbis-Bettman, p.26; Hutchison Library, p.23, p.22 (Sarah Errington); Mary Evans Picture
Library, p.15; Panos Pictures, pp.20, 21 (Peter Barker); Redferns, pp.14, 28; Reg Wilson, p.29;
Trip, pp.10, 18 (D. Butcher), p.11 (J. Okwesa); Zefa, pp.5, 7, 12, 16, 25, p.24 (J. Schorken).

Cover photograph: Redferns

Our thanks to Betty Root for her comments in the preparation of this book.

Every effort has been made to contact copyright holders of any material reproduced in
this book. Any omissions will be rectified in subsequent printings if notice is given to the
Publisher.

CONTENTS

Some words are shown in bold, **like this**.
You can find out what they mean by looking
in the Glossary.

INTRODUCTION

Music is very important in most religions. This book tells you about some of the different musical instruments which are used in services and other kinds of worship in religions across the world. It is also about ways of singing in worship, because many more people join in worship by singing rather than by playing instruments.

The voice is the most important 'instrument' in religious music

This Jewish rabbi is playing a traditional horn called a shofar

You will probably recognise some of the instruments and singing styles in this book, as well as the places where they are used. Some of them will be new to you. But they are all used to help people worship in different religions around the world.

THE CHRISTIAN CHOIR AND CONGREGATION

There is often a choir in a Christian church. A choir is a group of singers who help the congregation to sing the hymns and psalms.

Singing is an important part of Christian worship

The people who sing in the church choir are called choristers

The singers in the choir will be divided up according to whether their voices are high or low. The choir will often include children because they can sing higher **notes** than adults. The congregation are the people who come to worship in the church. They enjoy singing together with the choir.

GREGORIAN CHANT

Gregorian **chant** is a very old way of singing used by the Roman Catholic Church. It uses only a small number of **notes** and the singers all sing the same notes. It is often sung by people in **religious orders**.

Gregorian chanting often takes place in monastery chapels like this one

These monks are chanting

Gregorian chant is very simple and gentle because the singers believe this shows respect for God. Many people in the busy world of today like listening to Gregorian chant because it is so peaceful.

THE GOSPEL CHOIR

The best-known kind of Gospel music is the kind sung by choirs in Pentecostal churches in America, particularly by African-American people. It is very exciting music which shows the joy of worshipping God. It has lots of lively tunes and strong **rhythms**.

There are often many singers in a Gospel choir

These singers belong to a Gospel choir

Gospel singers often clap their hands and play **percussion** instruments while they sing. In churches a pianist or organist will usually play when the choir sings. Gospel music is also performed in concert halls.

JEWISH MUSIC

A Jewish place of worship is called a synagogue. There will often be a choir who will sing **sacred texts** and songs. An especially gifted singer will often sing a **solo** part in the music. This person is called a cantor.

A Jewish cantor

This choir is singing in a Jewish synagogue

There is a very old **tradition** of singing in the Jewish religion. There are special kinds of singing for different ceremonies and for certain special occasions in a person's life.

THE ORGAN AND HARMONIUM

The organ is an instrument often found in churches. It is played using a set of **keyboards** and **pedals**. Its sound comes from big pipes. Air is pushed into the pipes by **bellows**. Today the bellows are powered by electricity, but years ago they had to be pumped by hand. The organ has a loud, powerful sound.

This organist is playing an organ in a church

The harmonium is a smaller type of organ

The harmonium is a small organ which uses metal **reeds** instead of pipes to make a sound. Air is pushed through the reeds by bellows. It is not often used today. Because it was small it was often taken by Christian **missionaries** to faraway countries to use when people sang hymns.

THE SALVATION ARMY

The Salvation Army is a worldwide Christian organisation. It encourages Christian beliefs and helps people in need. The Salvation Army has bands which play Christian music in public places. They will often use **brass** and **woodwind** instruments.

This Salvation Army Band is playing on a sea front

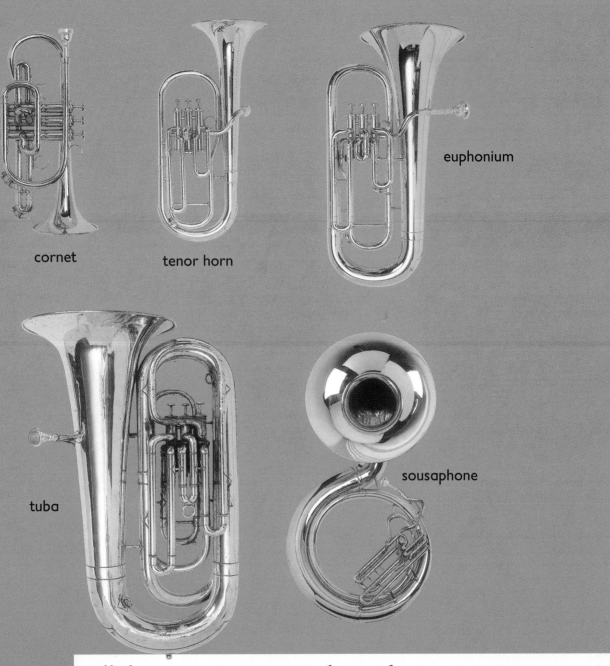

euphonium

cornet

tenor horn

tuba

sousaphone

All these instruments can be used in Salvation Army bands

You will often see Salvation Army bands playing music, such as **carols**, at Christmas time. While they play they may collect money from passers-by. The money is used to help people who are sick, hungry or have no home to live in.

CHRISTIAN ROCK AND FOLK MUSIC

Many Christians believe it is important to share their **faith** with as many people as possible. One way of doing this is by performing popular music, such as rock music, with a Christian message. They will use electric guitars, electric bass guitars, keyboard instruments, drums and microphones just like any other rock band.

The musicians in this rock band share the Christian faith

These musicians are playing folk music
at a Christian service

Many Christian worshippers enjoy informal folk music
worship without a choir or organ. Often a group of
singers with **acoustic** guitars will sing and play along with
the worshippers. This kind of music can be performed in
some churches, in halls or in people's homes.

MUSIC AT HINDU CEREMONIES

Special occasions in the **Hindu** religion, such as weddings, will often have music. Different kinds of music can be used, from **traditional** singing with instruments to Indian pop music and dancing. The music helps everyone to enjoy the ceremony.

This Hindu ceremony includes music

violin

flute

harmonium

lute

voice

barrel drums

Any of these instruments can be used
at a Hindu celebration

There are many different instruments being used at this
Hindu celebration, including barrel drums and an Indian
lute. A barrel drum has a strap so it can be played with
both hands. The Indian lute is a stringed instrument a bit
like a guitar.

TIBETAN TEMPLE MUSIC

Tibetan **Buddhism** is the main religion of Tibet and Mongolia. The monks who live in a Tibetan Buddhist temple are called lamas. Part of their worship is to **recite** Buddhist **scriptures** and **chant**. Tibetan chanting has a lot of low **notes**.

These Tibetan monks are performing in a Buddhist temple

These Tibetan lamas are playing trumpets

The lamas also play instruments which include trumpets and **percussion** instruments. Tibetan trumpets are made of metal. They can only play a few notes. They make a deep sound and can be heard a long way away.

JAPANESE TEMPLE MUSIC

The **traditional** religion of Japan is called Shinto. The religious music of Japan is called kagura which means 'god music'. The music is performed to make the gods pleased. New kagura music is still being written and performed in Japan.

These musicians are performing Japanese religious music

These kagura musicians are playing a very large drum

Kagura music includes singing and chanting. Drums, rattles and flutes are also played. The music is performed in temples and also at festivals and special occasions. The big drums used in kagura music make a loud, pounding sound. The drummers often play them very gracefully, as if they were dancing as they play.

NEW ORLEANS FUNERAL MUSIC

The city of New Orleans in the USA is said to be the place where **jazz** music began. It was started by African-American people. In New Orleans there are sometimes **traditional** jazz funerals in which a jazz band walks with the funeral procession playing sad, slow music.

A traditional New Orleans funeral procession

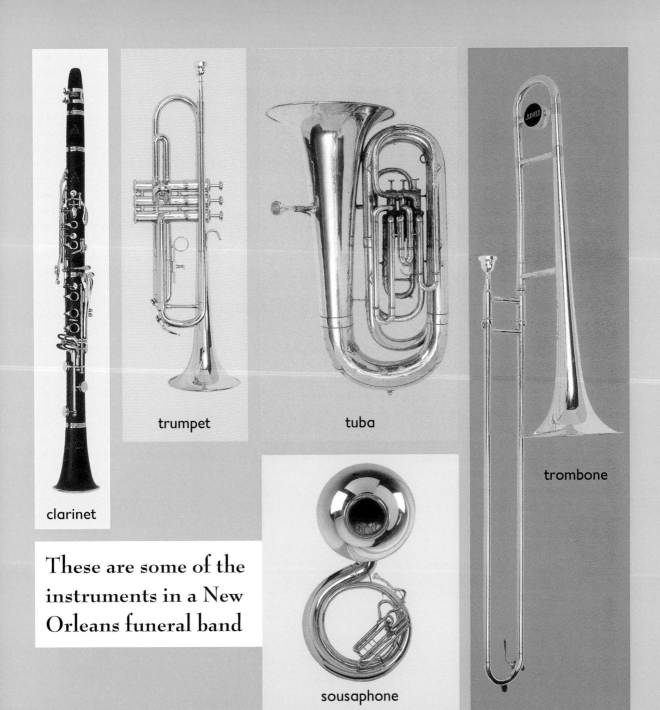

trumpet

tuba

trombone

clarinet

sousaphone

These are some of the instruments in a New Orleans funeral band

The instruments the band play will usually include a clarinet, which is a **reed** instrument. There will also usually be a trumpet, a trombone, and a tuba or sousaphone, which are all **brass** instruments. These instruments are all used in jazz and in marching band music as well.

CONCERT AND THEATRE MUSIC

Some types of Christian music, such as oratorios, are performed in concert halls as well as in church. This is usually because many people like to just listen to the music rather than it being an act of worship. An oratorio has a choir and **solo** singers. There can also be a classical orchestra of string, wind and **percussion** instruments and an organ or other **keyboard** instruments.

This orchestra, choir and solo singers are performing an oratorio

This scene is from the stage musical
Jesus Christ Superstar

There are several stage musicals based on religious stories. These mix pop and rock music with dancing and acting to tell the story. Many people enjoy them even if they do not share the religion in the story. The instruments used will often include rock guitars, keyboards and drums as well as classical instruments. There will be solo singers for the important parts and often a chorus of extra singers as well.

GLOSSARY

acoustic   instruments which do not have to be played through an electric amplifier

bellows   an air-tight pouch which forces air into an instrument when it is squeezed

brass   a type of hard metal used for making some wind instruments

Buddhism   an Eastern religion

carols   special Christian hymns and songs sung at Christmas

chant   a type of singing used in many world religions. It is usually slow and uses only a small number of different notes

faith   a set of religious beliefs. It can also mean the trust the believer places in them

Hindu   someone who is a member of the Hindu faith, a religion which started in India

jazz   a popular form of music started by African-American people about one hundred years ago

keyboards   electronic instruments played with keys like those of a piano or organ

missionaries   people who travel to other countries to spread their religious faith

notes   musical sounds

pedals   levers on an instrument which are pressed by the player's feet

percussion   instruments played by shaking or hitting

recite   to sing or speak words from memory

reed   thin strip of metal or cane which makes a sound when air is blown across it

religious orders   groups of people who live together, often very simply, to concentrate on worship

rhythms   the regular patterns of notes in music

sacred texts   written teachings and rules which are important in a religion

scriptures   written teachings and rules which are important in a religion

solo   one musician singing or playing

tradition   ways of doing things which have not changed for a long time

woodwind   reed wind instruments such as the clarinet, saxophone and oboe, and flutes

FURTHER READING

Live Music! Elizabeth Sharma. Wayland, 1992

You may need help to read these other titles on music.

Eyewitness Kit: Music. Dorling Kindersley, 1993

How the World Makes Music. Iwo Zaluski and Pamela Zaluski. Young Library, 1994

The World of Music: With CD. Nicola Barber and Mary Mure. Evans Brothers, 1994

INDEX